D0801623

COMMON SENSE

COMMON

Illustrations by Vicky Rabinowic

Ariel Books

Andrews and McMeel
Kansas City

SENSE

A Book of
Wit and Wisdom

ISBN: 0-8362-2645-3
Library of Congress Catalog Card Number:
96-85933

CONTENTS

COMMON SENSE

introduction

"USE your common sense," we are often told as children (and every now and then as adults). What does this advice—or admonition—mean? It means do what is sensible, what is prudent. Common sense is a form of wisdom, simply stated and readily understood. And so, if this wisdom is so simple, so apparent, why fill a book with it? Because, in the midst of our busy and complex lives, we may have forgotten to use our common sense. The words here, then, are a delightful reminder.

Uttered by philosophers, athletes, writers, and many plain folks, the statements, proverbs, and sayings collected here are both insightful and obvious; they all resonate with truth and, well, good sense. They are pearls of wisdom—or perhaps more accurately, diamonds in the rough. In our increasingly sophisticated world, it is comforting indeed to know that common sense is still in vogue.

Common sense is genius dressed in its working clothes.

—RALPH WALDO EMERSON

Happiness

Follow your bliss.
—JAMES CAMPBELL

Never work just for money or for power. They won't save your soul or help you sleep at night.
—MARIAN WRIGHT EDELMAN

The key to everything is patience.
You get the chicken by hatching the
egg—not by smashing it.

—Ellen Glasgow

If we had no winter, the spring would
not be so pleasant: If we did not sometimes taste of adversity, prosperity
would not be so welcome.

—Anne Bradstreet

COMMON SENSE

If you can't change your fate, change your attitude.

—AMY TAN

Before you marry keep both eyes open; after marriage shut one.

—JAMAICAN PROVERB

First say to yourself what you would be; and then do what you have to do.

—EPICTETUS.

Always leave something to wish for; otherwise you will be miserable from your very happiness.

—BALTASAR GRACIÁN

COMMON SENSE

Let me listen to me and not to them.

—GERTRUDE STEIN

Happiness is nothing but everyday living seen through a veil.
—ZORA NEALE HURSTON

The secret is keeping busy, and loving
what you do.
—LIONEL HAMPTON

Think of all the beauty still left
around you and be happy.
—ANNE FRANK

Happiness is good health and a bad
memory.
—INGRID BERGMAN

Happiness for the average person may be said to flow largely from common sense—adapting oneself to circumstances—and a sense of humor.
—BEATRICE LILLIE

Sometimes small things lead to great joys.
—SAMUEL JOSEPH AGNON

COMMON SENSE

Find out what you like doing best and
get someone to pay you for doing it.
—KATHERINE WHITEHORN

Happiness? A good cigar, a good
meal, a good cigar, and a good
woman—or a bad woman; it depends
on how much happiness you can
handle.

—GEORGE BURNS

Our greatest glory is not in never
falling but in rising every time we fall.

—CONFUCIUS,

My creed is that:
Happiness is the only good.
The place to be happy is here.
The time to be happy is now.
The way to be happy is to make
others so.

—ROBERT G. INGERSOLL

For the happiest life, days should be rigorously planned, nights left open to chance.
—MIGNON MCLAUGHLIN

The moments of happiness we enjoy take us by surprise. It is not that we seize them, but that they seize us.
—ASHLEY MONTAGU

Say "I love you" to those you love.
The eternal silence is long enough to
be silent in, and that awaits us all.

—GEORGE ELIOT

COMMON SENSE

Happiness: a good bank account, a good cook, and a good digestion.

—JEAN-JACQUES ROUSSEAU

Mingle a little folly with your wisdom; a little nonsense now and then is pleasant.

—HORACE

The best way to make your dreams
come true is to wake up.

—PAUL VALÉRY

Remember that happiness is a way of
travel—not a destination.

—ROY M. GOODMAN

Think contentment the greatest
wealth.

—GEORGE SHELLEY

There is only one way to happiness and that is to cease worrying about things which are beyond the power of our will.

—EPICTETUS

When one door of happiness closes, another opens; but often we look so long at the closed door that we do not see the one which has been opened for us.

—HELEN KELLER

A man hath no better thing under the sun than to eat, and to drink, and to be merry.

—ECCLESIASTES 8:15

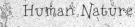

Human Nature

COMMON SENSE

It's better to keep one's mouth shut
and be thought a fool than to open it
and resolve all doubt.

—ABRAHAM LINCOLN

He that lies down with dogs, shall rise
up with fleas.

—BENJAMIN FRANKLIN

The fool wonders, the wise man asks.

—BENJAMIN DISRAELI

If you want to be respected by others the great thing is to respect yourself. Only by that, only by self-respect will you compel others to respect you.

—FYODOR DOSTOYEVSKY

A wise man makes his own decisions, an ignorant man follows the public opinion.

—CHINESE PROVERB

Before buying anything, it is well to ask if one could do without it.

—JOHN LUBBOCK

An open mind is all very well in its way, but it ought not to be so open that there is no keeping anything in or out of it. It should be capable of shutting its doors sometimes, or it may be found a little drafty.

—SAMUEL BUTLER

The person who knows "how" will always have a job. The person who knows "why" will always be his boss.

—DIANE RAVITCH

Don't worry about your originality. You could not get rid of it even if you wanted to. It will stick to you and show up for better or worse in spite of all you or anyone else can do.

—ROBERT HENRI

COMMON SENSE

Take time for all things: great haste
makes great waste.
—BENJAMIN FRANKLIN

Equals make the best friends.
—AESOP

If you want a thing done well, do it
yourself.
—NAPOLÉON BONAPARTE

When one is a stranger to oneself
then one is estranged from others too.
If one is out of touch with oneself,
then one cannot touch others.

—ANNE MORROW
LINDBERGH

Your heart often knows things before
your mind does.

—POLLY ADLER

COMMON SENSE

Nothing is particularly hard if you divide it into small jobs.

—RAY KROC

What we have to learn to do, we learn by doing.

—ARISTOTLE

There are some people that if they don't know, you can't tell them.

—LOUIS ARMSTRONG

The more people have studied different methods of bringing up children the more they have come to the conclusion that what good mothers and fathers instinctively feel like doing for their babies is the best after all.

—BENJAMIN SPOCK

If you want the present to be different from the past, study the past.

—BARUCH SPINOZA

Do you know the difference between education and experience? Education is when you read the fine print; experience is what you get when you don't.

—PETE SEEGER

Don't judge a man's wealth—or his piety—by his appearance on Sunday.

—BENJAMIN FRANKLIN

Experience is more convincing than logic.

—Isaac Abravanel

Before you borrow money from a friend, decide which you need more.

—Anonymous

Weigh the meaning and look not at the words.

—Ben Jonson

It's a wise man who profits by his own experience, but it's a good deal wiser one who lets the rattlesnake bite the other fellow.

—JOSH BILLINGS

Let us take men as they are, not as they ought to be.

—FRANZ SCHUBERT

COMMON SENSE

Trust everybody, but cut the cards.
—FINLEY PETER DUNNE

There are many forms of lunacy, but
only one kind of common sense.
—IBO PROVERB

Promote yourself but do not demote
another.
—ISRAEL SALANTER

We neither get better or worse as we get older, but more like ourselves.

—ROBERT ANTHONY.

It is better to be wise than to seem wise.

—ORIGEN

Before we blame, we should first see if we can't excuse.

—G. C. LICHTENBERG

COMMON SENSE

He that is good for making excuses is seldom good for anything else.

—BENJAMIN FRANKLIN

Those who do not depend on luck have less bad luck.

—YIDDISH FOLK SAYING

Life

COMMON SENSE

I take a simple view of living. It is keep your eyes open and get on with it.
—LAURENCE OLIVIER

When you can't solve the problem, manage it.
—ROBERT H. SCHULLER

Do not run too far, for you must return the same distance.
—MIDRASH RABBAH

The past is a ghost, the future a dream, and all we ever *have* is now.

—BILL COSBY.

Life is better than death, I believe, if only because it is less boring, and because it has fresh peaches in it.

—ALICE WALKER

There is no royal road to anything. One thing at a time, and all things in succession. That which grows slowly endures.

—J. G. HOLLAND

Do not believe hastily: what harm quick belief can do.

—OVID

Don't fight a battle if you don't gain anything by winning.

—GENERAL GEORGE S. PATTON JR.

Pick battles big enough to matter, small enough to win.

—JONATHAN KOZOL

COMMON SENSE

Like an ox-cart driver in monsoon season or the skipper of a grounded ship, one must sometimes go forward by going back.

—JOHN BARTH

Even if you are on the right track, you'll get run over if you just sit there.

—WILL ROGERS

If you wish to learn the highest truths,
begin with the alphabet.

—JAPANESE PROVERB.

The best time to do a thing is when it
can be done.

—WILLIAM PICKENS

COMMON SENSE

Don't smoke too much, drink too much, eat too much or work too much. We're all on the road to the grave—but there's no reason to be in the passing lane.

—ROBERT ORBEN

Good judgment comes from experience. Experience comes from bad judgment.

—MARK TWAIN

Take voyages. Attempt them. There's nothing else.

—TENNESSEE WILLIAMS

Remember, a closed mouth gathers no foot.

—STEVE POST

COMMON SENSE

Think in the morning.
Act in the noon.
Eat in the evening.
Sleep in the night.

—WILLIAM BLAKE

*A*s one goes through life one learns
that if you don't paddle your own canoe,
you don't move.

—KATHARINE HEPBURN

Don't look back. Something might be gaining on you.

—SATCHEL PAIGE

Don't learn the tricks of the trade. Learn the trade.

—ANONYMOUS

Train your head and hands to do, your head and heart to dare.

—JOSEPH SEAMON
COTTER JR.

Minds are like parachutes: They only function when open.

—THOMAS DEWAR,

COMMON SENSE

Draw your salary before spending it.
—GEORGE ADE

It's all right to hold a conversation, but you should let go of it now and then.
—RICHARD ARMOUR

Everything changes but change.
—ISRAEL ZANGWILL

In a total work, the failures have their
not unimportant place.
—MAY SARTON

To think is not enough; you must
think of something.
—JULES RENARD

COMMON SENSE

The time to repair the roof is when the sun is shining.
—JOHN F. KENNEDY

First you should put together your
house, then your town, then the world.
—ISRAEL SALANTER LIPKIN

He who is not courageous enough to take risks will accomplish nothing in life.

—Muhammad Ali

The best way out is always through.

—Robert Frost

Never reach out your hand unless you're willing to extend an arm.

—Elizabeth Fuller

When you clench your fist, no one can put anything in your hand, nor can your hand pick up anything.

—ALEX HALEY

There are two ways of meeting difficulties: You alter the difficulties or you alter yourself to meet them.

—PHYLLIS BOTTOME

I don't know the key to success, but the key to failure is trying to please everybody.

—BILL COSBY

Success is more a function of consistent common sense than it is of genius.

—AN WANG

Don't accept that others know you
better than yourself.
—SONJA FRIEDMAN,

Life is too short to make an over-
serious business out of it.
—LIN YUTANG

Never tell a lie, but the truth you don't
have to tell.
—GEORGE SAFIR

COMMON SENSE

Never cut what you can untie.
—JOSEPH JOUBERT

Begin somewhere; you cannot build a reputation on what you intend to do.
—LIZ SMITH

Never let the fear of striking out get in your way.
—GEORGE HERMAN ("BABE") RUTH

How far you go in life depends on your being tender with the young, compassionate with the aged, sympathetic with the striving, and tolerant of the weak and the strong. Because someday in life you will have been all of these.

—GEORGE WASHINGTON
     CARVER

What really matters is what you do with what you have.

—SHIRLEY LORD

It is not so important to be serious as it is to be serious about the important things.

—ROBERT MAYNARD HUTCHINS

You know more of a road by having traveled it than by all the conjectures and descriptions in the world.

—WILLIAM HAZLITT

Don't throw away the old bucket until
you know whether the new one holds
water.

— SWEDISH PROVERB

In matters of conscience, first thoughts
are best; in matters of prudence, last
thoughts are best.

—ROBERT HALL

It's only when we truly know and
understand that we have a limited time
on earth—and that we have no way of
knowing when our time is up—that
we will begin to live each day to the
fullest, as if it was the only one we had.

—ELISABETH KÜBLER-ROSS

I have found out that friendship is quite as important as love and it isn't any easier than love.

—BRIGITTE BARDOT

Life comes in clusters, clusters of solitude, then a cluster when there is hardly time to breathe.

—MAY SARTON

Never take counsel of your fears.

—ANDREW JACKSON

When in doubt, do without.
—VISCOUNT HERBERT SAMUEL

Be careful what you show—and what you don't show.
—MARLENE DIETRICH

Life was meant to be lived, and curiosity must be kept alive. One must never, for whatever reason, turn his back on life.
—ELEANOR ROOSEVELT